Not Another Nun Story

Margaret Bolton

Not Another Nun Story

Acknowledgements

Grateful thanks to the Sisters of Mercy who took me into their fold
for six years, and offered life-changing experiences.
Particular thanks to Sister Catherine Seward for clarifying my memory
and providing the group photographs,
and to Sister Patricia Pak Poy for being a pin-up nun for many long years.

Thanks to my parents, who gave me the freedom to enter the convent
even though it wasn't their dream for me.
And thanks to Dheera, Jim and Simon, my siblings,
and Nicki, Craig and Narelle, my children,
for listening and encouraging.

Thanks to Stephen Matthews of Ginninderra Press,
who thought that these stories might be worth publishing.

And thanks to Sharon Kernot for her encouragement
and Ann Cotton for her proofreading.

Blessings on you all!

Not Another Nun Story
ISBN 978 1 74027 651 1
Copyright © Margaret Bolton 2010

First published 2010
Reprinted 2015

GINNINDERRA PRESS
PO Box 3461 Port Adelaide SA 5015
www.ginninderrapress.com.au

Contents

Introduction

Early in the morning on a February day in 1963, I entered the convent. Even earlier that morning, ten other young women had entered the convent.

Mum and I had come down from the country the previous day and stayed at the CWA hostel overnight. Our pre-booked taxi failed to materialise on time, and Mass was already well underway when we rang the front doorbell of the convent. Mum was shooshed away with hardly a chance for a decent goodbye. I quickly changed into postulant's clothing and was shown my seat in the chapel. Highly conscious of all eyes on the one who dared to be late right at the outset, a thought flitted through my mind, 'What the hell are you doing here, Margaret?' But it wasn't until six years later that I left.

When it came time to choose a religious name, my biblical pin-up was Simon of Cyrene, the guy from far away Africa who found himself commandeered to help Jesus carry his cross to Golgotha. 'But we can't let you be Sister Simon,' said the novice mistress. 'The students will call you Simple Simon.' So I settled for Cyrena, and the kids called me 'Sizey', which I guess was more apt for me than 'Simple'.

In the 1960s, convent life was positively antiquated, much as portrayed by Audrey Hepburn in the film *The Nun's Story*. The reforms of Vatican II were beginning to be implemented as I left.

I was still seventeen when I entered, straight after a two-year stint at boarding school. I was a very immature and naive country bumpkin. In that era, all nuns taught in the various schools of the order, except for a few who did domestic work. I studied for a university degree and taught part-time for all of those years. Having procured a scholarship after my second year at university and realising that an extra year wouldn't intrude upon the convent finances, I also completed an Honours course.

The following stories were written some twenty years after I left, then put in a box waiting another twenty years for an inclination to finish them.

Postulants with postulant mistress, 1963.
I'm first left in back row.

The Question of Why

Many factors were probably influential in my decision to enter the convent. Overtly I wanted to live for God, to be involved in God's work in some way. Most religious orders of the time were teaching orders, and that suited me.

My last two years of school were not really happy ones. We lived at Port Augusta at a time when country schools only went to Leaving standard, so students had to go to the city to do Leaving Honours. My mother sent me to a Catholic girls' boarding school, whereas I wanted to join my friends living in a hostel at Enfield and attending the local high school. The school she chose (no doubt the one with the most affordable fees) only went to Leaving standard, but had a sister school in the city that offered Leaving Honours. There were three of us who boarded at one campus but attended classes at the other. We wore the green uniform of the boarding school while the other 500 students wore the purple of the day school. So we stuck out like sore thumbs. And the other students in our class shunned us because of it. I thought it was because of who I was, not because of what I wore. So I finished day school with a less than healthy self-esteem that was compounded by failing Leaving Honours the first time I tried. At boarding school, my plain and simple country-girl image didn't wash with most of the other boarders, who were quite socially adept and well-to-do and, when not in uniform, dressed in a manner that befitted their station.

I guess in some ways the decision to enter was also influenced by the fact that I had a cousin about my age who had spent a couple of years at the St Joseph's Juniorate (it was like a boarding school for girls who wanted to become nuns). It wasn't too far from where we lived at that time so our family used to visit her every now and then. My father thought that my cousin was just the ant's pants – pretty, outgoing, full of laughter and fun to be with. Would entering the convent fill my nominally Catholic father with similar pride for his own daughter?

So the convent seemed appealing; the nuns were looked up to and respected. I would show all of them that I had what it took to be successful at least in that sphere.

But the understanding of these motivations didn't surface for many years after I had left. And really I didn't know God at all at that time. He (and it was 'He' then) was mighty and wonderful, to be awed and revered and to be prayed to, but in no way was God concerned with Margaret at all.

So with my brand-new *Summa Theologica* by Thomas Aquinas (given to me by my only two boarding school friends) and my prayer book packed in my suitcase, off I went, a bit like a lamb to the slaughter, really.

Easter Alleluias

On every day of our religious lives, nuns were expected to spend half an hour in meditation. The time set aside for this was first thing in the morning. Getting up at 5.25 a.m. never came easy for me. Whether in the cold and dark of a winter's morning, or the chill crisp autumn dawn when the sun was rising from the tinted east, or in the soothing cool before a hot summer's day, the only thing I could think of was sleep – my whole body cried out for more of it.

Little wonder then that my automatic response to this time of stillness and quiet was a soporific one. Even sitting bolt upright in the hard choir stall, I could only succumb to this overwhelming need. Remember that being a university student gave me the privilege of being allowed to stay up after lights out to complete required study – being a last-minute person, this often necessitated stints that didn't end till 2 a.m. or later.

This situation was compounded by a lack of instruction on how to meditate or what to do in meditation time. Vague instructions like 'read a passage of scripture and bring it to life by using your imagination' did nothing for me. It was obvious that meditation was considered to be an instinctual ability, an innate part of one dedicated to God. It was patently obvious that I'd missed out on this one – a failure in the contemplative realm. However, except for the constantly nodding head (I never actually fell off the choir stall), this failure never needed to be admitted, even to myself, let alone disclosed to others. I guess God was aware of it, but we kept it between ourselves. God never saw fit to inspire the novice mistress with this knowledge – I guess she was tied up in her own meditative world.

Sometimes, in the effort to stay awake, I would go outside and pace up and down the quadrangle. A whole new meaning to sleepwalking came into being. The clanking of our large and long rosary beads hanging from our belt added a soporific undercurrent, like the clacking of train wheels on railway tracks.

Browned off one Easter Sunday morning when the liturgical season proclaimed victory and resurrection in the face of my all too obvious failure, I decided that some surreptitious Handel might express proper Easter feelings. So with *The Messiah* tucked into my voluminous sleeves I wandered into the school courtyard and found a classroom with a record player connected to the outside sound system, and I let her rip.

Now Handel's 'Hallelujah Chorus' while sitting by a reeded and lilied fishpond from which misty vapours rose in that wonderfully autumn early morning chill as the sun rose to caress the world was an expression of prayer that I could fully enter into with ease and even be transported to some sort of mystic rapture. I could imagine the whole of heaven raising the roof in joyous praise of the risen Lord.

I guess I wasn't as far away from the chapel as I thought, and I guess I wasn't the only one moved by this great music, for by the end of the half hour many had joined me – not quite dancing in the streets but definitely dancing on the inside.

I eventually did get a handle on what meditation was all about – some ten years after leaving the convent.

Divine Office

Divine Office was one of the day's prayerful activities that I could get into and did like. There was no possibility of going to sleep, as we stood and chanted the hours of the Office.

Office was chanted five or six times a day. Matins and Lauds before Mass, and Prime after Mass but before breakfast. Terce, Sext and None (the third, sixth and ninth hours) came together at lunch time, with Vespers before tea and Compline before retiring at night. If in school at the time, Terce, Sext and None had to be 'made up' privately later in the day.

This was an ancient and universal tradition of the Church to mark the hours of the day with praise of our God. Psalms were recited or chanted with short antiphons before and after each psalm. Small Bible readings were read and prayers prayed. The content varied with the season so that the great psalms of praise were sung at Easter and Christmas and the songs of the humble, the downtrodden and sad were sung during Lent. In Advent the O Antiphons featured – O Wisdom, O Rod of Jesse's stem, O Dayspring from on high, O Desire of the nations, O Emmanuel. Advent with its purple hues and themes of longing and yearning has always been my favourite season.

Chanting was on a monotone but certainly not monotonous. We took turns in intoning the antiphons and reading the prayers, and the two sides of the chapel took turns in chanting the verses. Some who were tone-deaf produced some unusual patterns of monotone and pitch.

Although the Psalms were written well over two thousand years ago, their thoughts and emotions still resonate today. The gory bits such as 'May your children be dashed against the rocks' were omitted.

However, moods of course weren't constant and didn't always match the day's theme; at least, mine didn't. I could be singing about the mighty God who saves us from our foes when struggling with superiors or other sisters, about being caught in the miry mud at the bottom of a well when things were travelling along nicely, about the exultation of the greatness of a loving God when struggling with the injustices that life seemed to dish out to the whole world, about the joy of serving in our God's sanctuary when all I wanted to do was to go home.

Sometimes the Office served as an equaliser of thoughts and emotions when an equaliser was needed. I really came to treasure the Psalms with all their human emotions about God and about life.

The 'Brides of Christ' Chapter

Now you'd have to agree, wouldn't you, that it wouldn't be a proper nun story without a chapter entitled 'Brides of Christ'. This is it, but a word of explanation first.

The fashion in spectacles in the early 1960s was for them to be framed strongly in black – remember Nana Mouskouri? Nun-style spectacles at that time were frameless except for the minimal amount of wire necessary to hold the glass together. The thicker the glasses, the worse it looked. Mine were thick – very thick! Such a fashion was considered to be totally awful then, even though thirty years later it became popular.

Postulants wore their worldly glasses, proper nuns wore the rimless variety. The transition took place during the ceremony of Reception into the Congregation, when the full habit and veil were donned for the first time. This was the day we got to be brides of Christ.

A large wardrobe in the novice mistress's office housed a fairly wide selection of real and quite beautiful wedding gowns and veils that had been bequeathed by new and pious Catholic wives (probably nuns' sisters). I was somewhat astounded and absolutely delighted to find one of a larger size that both fitted me and looked, in my humble opinion, great! Like any bride on her wedding day, this was the crowning moment of the relationship.

It was quite some time afterwards, maybe ten or fifteen years, that I wrote two pieces in an attempt to excavate the pivotal question of the spectacles on that occasion, to see it in its full context, and to come to terms with it. Like an archaeologist bringing buried treasure into the clear light of today when all they'd previously known had been the crumbling distortion.

A fairy tale

Once upon a time there was a poor peasant girl, but this was only a disguise. She was really a beautiful princess. But so complete was her disguise that she'd forgotten about ever having been a princess. Even the glasses she wore gave no sight of her true self. But when the prince rode by on his marvellous white steed, he knew straight away what she really was, and loved her. He loved her so much that he wanted her to be his, he wanted to share his love, his life and his wealth with her and make her happy for ever. The peasant girl was very flattered by his attentions and said she'd marry him, even though she knew deep in her heart that peasant girls weren't worthy of princes. He gave her a beautiful white gown with lace and beads, little white shoes and a golden tiara for the betrothal ceremony that was to take place in the most beautiful church in all the land.

She put on the fine clothes and felt like a princess and when she looked in the mirror she saw the reflection of a princess. But before she could be transformed into this princess, her wicked stepmother took away the crystal glasses and replaced them with crudely fashioned wire that only held plain glass through which dreams are only dreamt and never come true, for they are forgotten before awakening, And so she never became a real princess after all and could never really accept all the prince offered her in life. She withdrew into the peasant girl image and the prince was sad.

The true story

The novice mistress took away the glasses that matched the outfit that made me feel like a beautiful bride. I had been so thrilled to actually look beautiful for that occasion that was momentarily so symbolic of all that the outfit stood for: beauty, integrity, beloved, forever – 'He is mine and I am his' (Song of Songs). And she made me wear the wire-framed thick lenses that spoke only of the myopic, the ugly, the self-conscious, the nondescript, the not-appropriate; and in the wearing was the reality.

'Bride of Christ', December 1963.

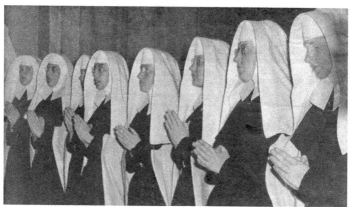

Sisters of Mercy, December 1963. That's me, second from right.

And I was angry, I was sad, I was disillusioned. I felt incomplete, an enigma, conspicuous – there, but not part of it.

But obedience and humility were the words of the day, and not one iota of that was expressed, because the novice mistress had to be obeyed, the bishop couldn't be kept waiting, family mustn't be disappointed, others in white were agog and aglow, and pride was a sin. And crosses, after all, Cyrena, were for carrying.

Don't Let It Go To Your Head

Long before feminists made statements about their identity by refusing to shave their armpits and legs, and just as guys were beginning to make statements about their identity by letting their hair grow into long curly locks that could be tied into ponytails, religious sisters were making statements about their identity as non- (oops, nun-) women by shaving their heads.

No doubt you've seen Audrey Hepburn in *The Nun's Story* having her locks chomped off by the novice mistress when she first donned full habit. And yes, that's just how it was, only it was the second-year novice who was supposed to look after you rather than the novice mistress who did the dastardly deed. And in the name of humility I remained stoically unmoved by this ritual but secretly cried my heart out when left alone to sweep up the evidence from the floor.

Despite the fact that I outwardly concurred with the opinion that it was much more comfortable and healthier to have no hair under all that head gear in the height of summer, I never really got quite used to this loss; I never really stopped secretly grieving for a coiffure and all its accoutrements of shampoo, rollers, hairspray, ribbons, clips and the like.

In fact, I was secretly often too busy, too preoccupied, perhaps even too engrossed in catching up on my prayers, to attend to the obligatory weekly ritual of shaving the head. And while head coverings were created and worn on every occasion when the veil and coif were removed (like night caps for bed, shower caps for bathing and bathing caps for swimming), all these were really worn to hide the fact that underneath it all a secret garden of hairiness was being cultivated. Constant vigilance was required to disguise an escaping lock. Shortness correlates with curliness on my head, so wisps couldn't be passed off as six o'clock shadows or as anything else but what they were. At least fairness of hue was on my side.

A decision to leave the convent could never be made in haste for it required a postponement of a few months in order that at least a presentable head of hair could be grown. Stray wisps were often the first telltale sign of a colleague's intention to leave, for such an action was always carried out in secret. Usually we didn't find out that she was leaving until she had gone.

But then Vatican II changed all that. The nuns shall look more ordinary, they said, while under their ecclesiastical breaths they probably added, and less like something out of a horror movie. Nuns shall stop hiding their femininity, they said, when they really meant that nuns had been denying it, and perhaps that was the reason for it all.

The post-Vatican transition from habits to street clothes was gradual and via several intermediary steps. The first was to reveal a fringe or a first flurry of curls. Only at the front, mind you. A modified veil still covered the rest. What a shock to see older sisters' hair colour and characteristics for the first time. What a shock for older sisters to find that despite not having had any for all those years, it was now grey. But not the Mother Provincial's – hers stayed a fiery red with only a hint of ageing paleness. Now there's some subconscious resistance for you – and I'd always taken her for a model of piety.

Civil War On the Kitchen Floor

The first novitiate year was a time for testing one's vocation and undergoing a rigorous initiation into religious life.

This was the year when ordinary life, teaching in schools or studying to teach in schools, was suspended. Forays beyond the convent walls were limited to weekly walks to either a church in a neighbouring suburb or to the West Terrace Cemetery to weed the graves of those sisters who had gone before us.

A program of prayer, study and manual labour was the order of the day. First-year novices kept the house running – they did the kitchen chores, polished the chapel floor (yes, on hands and knees), looked after the refectory, laundered the linen and starched the coifs. They were cut off not only from the wider world but also from the rest of the nun-world.

Kitchen duty was perhaps the most onerous and time-consuming – the least welcomed – of the rostered duties. The actual cooking itself was done by older and wiser nuns experienced in large-scale culinary arts and in the skill of ensuring that novices learnt to be humble.

One of the rituals that occurred each day was that the kitchen and adjoining scullery (wash-up room) floors were washed five minutes before the lunchtime stampede of sisters beating a path to the refectory. But to save the desired outcome of washing the floor being completely reversed, a newspaper trail was laid like stepping stones across a creek. The trick for the novice was to get it just right before the hordes arrived who seemed hell-bent on leaving behind their muddy footprints. They too valued humility in novices, for hadn't they once learnt in the same school?

But there is a bright side to every coin and even this ritual had

one small compensation. If she could read fast enough, a novice could actually catch up with what was going on in the world as she slowly and carefully positioned the paper suitably on the floor.

The year that I was a first-year novice my father, the policeman, bored with life in a slack country town, had volunteered for duty as part of the United Nations police force keeping the peace between warring factions of Greeks and Turks on the island of Cyprus. I was naturally anxious about his safety in the thick of things over there, an anxiety heightened by an active imagination functioning in the absence of factual information. My worst fears came to fruition one day when laying the kitchen floor with the front page of *The Advertiser*, whose headlines splashed the news of out and out civil war, guns and all, and with little regard for the blue berets of the United Nations.

It was difficult to serve the silently eating community or to stand in line to wash dinner plates in a manner that hid the upheaval of emotions deep within. A walk-in broom cupboard offered some sort of refuge – out of sight, but not out of earshot; sobbing is difficult to completely quash.

Sister Cecilia found me there, and offered comforting arms, a shoulder to lean on, a willing ear and a large white handkerchief. But Sister Cecilia was a community sister and so off limits, out of bounds. She and I entered into a silent conspiracy about this closeted meeting, and every morning thereafter in the same cupboard, neatly folded and hidden under the tin of floor polish there miraculously appeared all relevant newspaper articles. For a whole year I was able to follow events in Cyprus until my father came safely home.

Sister Cecilia to this day remains a friend.

All the Eggs In the Basket

In my teenage years I developed a habit of clumsiness in response to feelings of inadequacy. 'Like a bull in a china shop' was a saying muttered frequently in my direction in those days. This disposition accompanied me into the convent as well.

I was a university student all of the time I was there (except the first novitiate year). Our convent was in the city, within walking distance of the campus, and so walking was how we got there. A bag of heavy books toted daily created tensions in my back and shoulder muscles that could be temporarily relieved by dropping the bag while waiting at traffic lights. Spontaneous dropping had more immediate effects than careful placing, and soon became an ingrained habit.

A retreat before renewing vows at Christmas time meant two weeks of return to kitchen duty interspersed among prayers and sermons about a mythical character called Matilda McTwiggetty, thinly disguised as a model religious.

A newly arrived load of eggs needed transferring from the kitchen to the cellar where they were stored in the cool darkness. Two baskets full, one with and one without a handle. I volunteered, but with my reputation the cook in her wisdom ordered me to find someone else to take them down. Gently protesting with my disarming smile, I won her over to my way of thinking and with a heightened consciousness set off down the cellar steps, with one basket cradled under my left arm, the other suspended from my right. Such was my care that everything went well during the descent.

A wire gate at the bottom needed unlatching. Involuntarily and habitually, the right-hand basket received the same treatment as my heavily loaded satchel at the traffic lights.

I had imbibed a modicum of humility by this time, so I went to face the music. To this day I'm sure I was the only nun ever to be completely banned from the kitchen again.

And needless to say, I did not – and I repeat, did not – remain lifelong friends with *Soeur La Cook*.

Enfranchisement

I had my twenty-first birthday in the convent and so was entitled to vote in the next parliamentary election (the age of majority was lowered to eighteen at a later date).

The first election of my enfranchisement took place at a time when we had little contact with the wider world and its communications. We had no access whatever to election speeches or discussion, either in the flesh or via the media. And politics was one of the *verboten* subjects of conversation at recreation times.

Determined to be fiercely independent in exercising this right for the first time, I eschewed my parents' liberal values and the Church's preferred option of the DLP. I think I had unconsciously imbibed suspicions that the Labor Party might be infiltrated by communists, and this despite, or perhaps confirmed by, my sister's sharing of some of her insights into Marxism gained by studying politics. In those days before the Democrats, this left little alternative but to vote informal. (How I cringe at all this now!)

So I fronted up to the Town Hall to have my name marked on the electoral roll. It felt peculiar using my secular name again – it was one of the things 'put off' in the putting on of the religious habit. I collected my papers, went into the little booth to be secreted from other voters, pretended to mark the little squares, neatly folded up the ballot paper with its still empty boxes and deposited them in the ballot box.

I did feel uneasy about this course of action, but consoled myself that religious people were in the world but not of it and so it didn't really matter anyway.

A few weeks later, news of the election results filtered through our protective screen. The Labor Party had been victorious after all. Perhaps if I'd even done the donkey thing I could have averted such a tragedy. And so experiential learning taught that not only did voting matter, but also that it was important to be properly informed about all political parties. By the next election I had discovered that Don Dunstan wasn't such a bad guy after all.

Family Matters

My family, just before I entered the convent.

While the ultimate pride and pinnacle of success of every Catholic family in the 1960s and before was to bring to birth and nurture a vocation, if not a priestly one then at second-best a religious one, when it came to the crunch it was the family perhaps even more than the religious-to-be that paid the highest price. For that separation from the world entailed in entering religious life included putting aside one's parents and siblings as if they never mattered. At least the would-be-religious freely chose such a path; the family could only acquiesce. Theirs was the greater sacrifice.

Some parents found it more difficult to cope with than if their child had died – a kind of living death that went on and on inexorably.

My mother wasn't Catholic so did not have the sense of pride to offset the sacrifice. But we'd been encouraged to be independent and our decisions were stood by. Still my mother must have bid goodbye at the convent door on that fateful morning with more than a lump in her throat, especially given the bigotry displayed by her own family when she married a Catholic.

During the novitiate years, a monthly visit of one hour was allowed. Mostly these were joyous and eagerly anticipated events. There were some parents who strongly opposed their daughter's decision to follow their vocation (even to the extent that the daughters had to wait until they were twenty-one before entering). Their continued resistance was expressed by not visiting at all or by spending the whole hour in loud berating or public tantrums.

None of this was my experience as the family lived at Port Pirie and later Whyalla, too far to pop in on a Sunday afternoon for an hour. I was thrilled that they made the trip to be with me for the celebration of my twenty-first birthday, which I shifted to Easter Sunday of that year, as Good Friday would have been the most uncelebratory day in the conventual calendar year.

Letters became precious. My mother continued her weekly news bulletins that she'd been so faithful to while we were at boarding school. My very much younger brother started school, learnt to write and often popped a sentence and a drawing in with Mum's to this sister who he hardly knew as he had only been two when I went to boarding school. My father spent a year in Cyprus, during which he also visited the Holy Land and other surrounding areas. Wonderfully descriptive and evocative letters with even more exquisite photos arrived regularly. My sister was studying at the same university during my later years in the convent and lived within the city precincts. However, for her, it wasn't cool to be visiting nunneries.

Vatican II encouraged nuns to reclaim family connections and to go home for visits as part of becoming more real. Who could forget that first Christmas when after lunch with community the nuns were allowed to go home for the afternoon and the evening meal, and to be seen eating again! For some it was the first time they had seen the house to which their family had moved since they left home.

I suppose there were half a dozen of us whose families lived too far away for us to join this freedom ride. Several sisters had invited me

The plane trip over was eventless. Left Sydney at ... just short of the Turkey-Iran border. Longest night in the world!! lovely ... plane - 600 mph or 56,000' outside temperature -47°C.

AUSTRALIAN POLICE CONTINGENT
UNFICYP
CIVILIAN POLICE
Box 1767
NICOSIA
CYPRUS.

Monday 1st June

Sr. Mary Cyrena
Dear Mary,
    I said I would and I did. Here we are in sunny Cyprus and a fabulous world where everything is the same as home but oh so different, a tradition and national mores and way of life that comes from thousands? of years of being a melting pot of the fabled races of the area — the Biblical nations, the Romans, Abyssinians, Byzantium and Greece and Muslim and Venetian and the French Lusignans. Ruins and churches and pottery, glass, silver and leather, sculpture and stone axes of neolithic age; folk lore and dancing, music and national costumes, customs and the east meeting the west. Old old cathedrals in marvellous Gothic stone, carted by slaves and cut by men of all nations who left their craft marks on the stones; and lovely work done in 1100 B.C., columns ...

to join them but I would have felt an intruder in their first opportunity for domestic intimacy. I guess we six all felt a bereftness that needed to be nurtured in solitude. I know some of the others went to bed too. I, for one, caught up on some much-needed sleep. Perhaps I was beginning to imbibe some of that humility that enabled me to bury even my deepest feelings.

There did come a time, however, when I could visit Whyalla. Another nun had a dying relative in Whyalla and needed someone to accompany her. We slept in the convent with sisters of another order, but I could spend the days at home.

My teenage brother was into sailing yachts at the time, and my father was into building yachts for him to sail, so 'trying her out' was required of me. The eyes of the locals must have fairly popped to see the sign of the flying black veil along with the spinnaker.

On the same visit I was talked into taking my little brother for a swim. I had real problems of discernment about this action for it

Thank you letter from my brother on his fifth birthday.
He visited just before that and was taken with the baby mice
that one of the primary school teacher nuns was raising.
Unfortunately, the mother ate all her babies on the following day.

31

required divesting the habit and donning bathers and a bathing cap (for hirsuteness was still an issue), and the obligatory obedience required permission from a superior to be so daring. But on the pretext of what the eye didn't see, we went swimming. Whyalla waters were known for being too shallow for beach swimming so we went to the breakwater near the yacht club. My little brother assured me that Dad would get him into trouble if he went over his depth as he couldn't swim, so I assured him that Dad probably wouldn't mind if I was there. I hopped in first. Before I could even surface, he had launched himself into the deep and into the vicinity of my arms, trusting that I would catch and sustain him. What a lesson in that sort of childlike trust that the gospel demanded!

When I came to leave the convent, I remember my mother's reaction to the news. 'Don't worry about a thing, dear,' she said. 'I've been saving a little nest egg for when this time came.' I wonder how long she had secretly hoped for this, or whether she knew intuitively that such a day would come.

Food, Glorious Food

The first thing I noticed about convent food was the goodness of it all. At home my mother struggled to make the money go around to feed, clothe and provide for four children. On entering the convent my standard of living was certainly raised several degrees, despite the vow of poverty. The excuse of 'an apple a day keeps the doctor away' was a saying that was extended to good food in general.

Everyday eating was fairly plain, meat and three veg, sometimes salad in the summer. Casseroles, curry and roasts included. Cooking for sixty people was always done in bulk, had to be completed by the time of the noon Angelus bell, and kept warm in the bain-marie till serving time at 12.30.

Breakfast at home had consisted of eggs when we had chooks, but just cereal and toast otherwise. In the convent we had an array of breakfast dishes to accompany the cereal and toast. Scrambled eggs, tripe, fricasseed lamb tongues, sausages and bacon – some new and exciting tastes for me, even though many hated them. The toaster cooked twelve slices of bread at once. It was a real juggling act to get the toast cooked in time without burning it.

The main meal was at lunchtime, but mine was heated up at teatime as I was often at uni for lunch. And tea was always similar to lunch, though perhaps lighter. No such thing as sandwiches, except to take to uni.

Meals were eaten in silence on most days. The midday meal was accompanied by readings from the Martyrology, accounts of the ultimate fate of martyrs, read on their feast days. This was gruesome enough to put anyone off eating too much, especially if the martyr ended up being roasted on the spit (St Laurence) or as someone else's lunch.

Easter, Christmas, the novice mistress and superior's feast days were occasions to live it up, and live it up we did. The range of delicate cakes and sweets was enormous, and we had to learn how to cook them in our novitiate year. Fruited jellies, wined trifles, brandy snaps, cream puffs, decorated cup cakes, creamed lilies, all of these graced the table along with the large iced celebratory fruit cake. No thoughts for the starving millions in this house.

Good Friday, on the other hand, had its own set of eating rules. For tea we had 'collation', a sauce concocted by adding arrowroot to the dregs of the altar wine collected over the year. On its own, not as an accompaniment to other food. And it was eaten while standing and in silence, which was in order for the whole day.

The Getting of Wisdom

It was again well into the Great Silence, and getting near to time for lights out. But the obligatory daily rosary hadn't yet been recited.

Reciting the rosary at the end of the day when eyes can hardly be held open and heads are apt to nod off requires a certain amount of rote that can only be provided by a companion. Any thought of accompanying meditation is nonsensical in this situation and why bother when not even laid down in the terms of the obligation.

Sister Stephen and I were sitting on the balcony and well into the third decade of the rosary when I entered into yet another huge yawn. But blow me down, if there wasn't quite an audible click and my mouth wouldn't shut. Talk about being caught in the act. After five minutes of desperate facial contortions without result, we realised that help needed to be sought.

With Stephen as my spokesnun, for it is difficult to make much sense talking with the jaw locked open, we, like Aaron and Moses before Pharoah, presented our dilemma.

Everyone had a cure for lockjaw.

Smack her hard on the back and the shock will fix it (that sounded awfully like its author was confused with hiccups).

Manipulate the jaw back into place (the trying hurt like hell but was totally ineffective).

Have a hot drink with plenty of honey to help it slide back into place (perhaps a variation of the honey, lemon and brandy that was standard for oncoming colds, and that hopefully staved off the dreaded Benadryl in the two-litre brown bottle that was standard once the cold had defied the brandy – or perhaps thrived on it).

Thrust a burning log into her face and the jolt of avoiding it would return the jaw to its normal position.

This was beginning to sound like a witch hunt and scared me off even listening to any other home-made remedies – all old wives' tales are dangerous, I concluded.

A doctor's visit was the only alternative. Unfortunately the novice mistress had to be woken up to call the doctor – she would surely put two and two together about the Great Silence. For just that minute or two, the inability to talk was a godsend!

Yes, the doctor would come on his way home from his late-night rounds. Probably be about an hour. Sitting in the cold parlour waiting. But when he arrived he was rather like God – kind, understanding and gentle of touch, requiring no explanation of how it had happened. I was praying that the novice mistress would follow his example when I was able to talk again.

My prayers were answered for once. She must have been plain tired for she went back to bed without a word, with the command that I do likewise. I guess perhaps she didn't want to be seen breaking the Great Silence although she must have been bursting to do so.

A couple of months later in the early morning, in the middle of Mass, when I was only bodily present being far away in the realm of the mind, bingo! another yawn ended up the same way. This time the nurse-nun did her best to restore me to normality but had a great deal of trouble in understanding my instructions delivered through the non-closing mouth. So again the doctor was summoned, but this time he wouldn't come until on his way to work.

Two hours to wait. Not only prayers but more importantly breakfast would have been and gone by then without me. And I still had a couple of classes to prepare for. Leaving things till the last minute sometimes has its drawbacks.

Not resigned to waiting for so long and frustrated that I hadn't been able to get intelligible instructions through to the nurse-nun, in anger (and silence) I shouted at her absent self in a demonstration that this was how you did it, you silly old bat, when my jaw responded to my manipulations and returned to its rightful position again.

And so on subsequent occasions I was able to put it back myself – no fuss.

It happened only a few times more, the last being after I'd left the convent and when driving the car in peak-hour traffic in Sydney. This presented its own difficulties in that combating lockjaw was a two-handed job.

A number of years later, on warning a dentist of such a possibility and, in the event, of my ability to fix it, I was informed that lockjaw can happen as a result of any significant change in the jaw line such as the removal or addition of a tooth or two. For me it had been the time of acquiring wisdom teeth.

Hospital Visitation

At one stage it was decided that Cyrena, now a fully fledged Sister of Mercy, should engage in one of the works of mercy, and so I was assigned to visit the Children's Hospital on Sunday mornings with a view to teaching religious education to the young Catholic patients. This was to be done on a one-to-one basis. It was rare to find a child who was even there two weeks running. Now, I ask you, what could be taught in one short lesson that might be of some value to the child?

I soon came to see that either the child came from a good Catholic family and went to a good Catholic school and so didn't need another 'lesson', or, at the other end of the spectrum, the word Catholic entered on their record in the square marked 'religion' indicated nominal and minimal involvement anyway and what difference could one ten-minute lesson about Jesus make to their life – a mere drop in the ocean.

I never looked forward to these Sunday morning visits – they were simply too hard, although once I got there, it wasn't so bad. Kids, even sick ones, are so engaging.

On one of these mornings, a girl of about seven was on my visiting list. The nurse-sister cautioned this nun-sister that she was not to tire this child as she was very sick, and my visiting time was limited to only a few minutes. I'll always remember vividly this child with the dark curly hair and pale wan face who lay so still, moving only her eyes in greeting. Any thought of a lesson was ludicrous in this situation. I wondered if she was dying and longed to hold her hand and tell her about meeting Jesus in heaven, but the words wouldn't come, and so, with just the promise to pray for her, I obeyed the nurse's orders willingly and moved on to the next child.

Later, on pondering my omission, I resolved to make up for it on the following Sunday – I even rehearsed in my mind what I could perhaps say to her. But when I got there she had died during the week. I was utterly sad.

Perhaps it was this little girl more than all the others who prompted me to abandon all thoughts of pious education. I found it easier all round and for all concerned to take my guitar rather than my books, and to sit on the Catholic kid's bed, gathering in any other kid in the ward regardless of religion to join me in song. My repertoire was very limited, but *Mary Poppins* and *The Sound of Music* were the flavours of the month. The kids certainly learnt their scales through 'Doe, a deer' and the song about the spoon full of sugar going down might have been especially written for these children. It wasn't very long before I found that Sunday mornings could be supercalifragilistic and sometimes even expialidocious.

The Burns Ward presented its own particular difficulties. A white hospital gown and mask had to be donned before entering this ward. What a sight – the white gown opening at the back over a voluminous black habit, and the mask covering what little of my face was free of coif and veil. I must have looked like a penguin in purdah. In the warmth of this ward, for the patients wore no clothes and no bed coverings that might subvert the healing process of burnt skin, my glasses kept continually fogging up as we sang together.

The hospital also threw at me my first experience with a very premature baby. So tiny, so wizened, how could it possibly survive? What was God on about in allowing such early births?

Flannel Flushing

I don't even remember what sparked it off, but it was after the time of the Great Silence when boisterous verbal outbursts were simply not an option.

The location was the shower block, the missile was a cold wet flannel and the target was taking refuge in the loo. In a quick movement from the throne, the object of my wrath avoided being hit as the dripping flannel flew over the top of the door. But like a homing pigeon, it found its resting place right in the middle of the loo bowl. Retrieval simply wasn't an option in the circumstances, and flushing was the only alternative – and done quick as a flash. No consideration of the consequences was entered into.

But in the cold dawn of early-morning prayer, the consequences became all too clear. A nun crime had been committed. Not only had Great Silence been broken, but unlawful and wanton disposal of an essential material possession had taken place. The vow of poverty had been compromised, the obligation to steward an essential *objet de vivre* had been violated.

Confession was in order. Not to the priest – the matter was not appropriate to that weekly ritual. But to the novice mistress in private. And she was under no obligation to represent the compassion, understanding and forgiveness of a loving God. She was there to see that you kept the rules and learnt humility. And what better way than to command you to expose your folly to the whole community in the Chapter of Faults.

You know about that too – that's when you kneel on your own in the middle of the chapel, announce your misdemeanour to the whole assembly and then fall prostrate on the floor in a gesture of abject humility.

OK, so I'd done all that before. I'd got used to the feeling. I'd mastered the physical gymnastics of lowering the body to a fully extended, face-down contact with the floor, and raising it again, so that I could do it with dignity and grace. And the other sisters must surely have been quite at home with my regular peccadilloes in relation to Great Silence.

But how on earth could I confess flushing a flannel down the dunny in a way that both articulated the truth and at the same time averted the possibility of bringing the house down in uncontrollable mirth?

Two By Two

Whenever we left the convent precincts, it had to be in pairs. When the whole group of novices went out walking, it looked like a scene from the Madeline books where there were twelve little girls in two straight lines.

OK, so we didn't go out all that often on foot. Except for the two of us who walked to uni and back each day. All would have been well if we both attended the same lectures, but hers was a science degree and mine an arts. A lot of time was on our hands, hanging around and waiting for each other.

Not only in pairs, but in silence. Difficult for me, but not for my companion – she found keeping the rules came naturally.

For a short while, a new postulant joined us in studying – she didn't see much point in silence either, but then she didn't last that long, leaving before the year was out.

In our final year at university, we shared a room together away from the rest of the sleeping quarters so that our midnight oil wouldn't disturb anyone. By the time midnight passed, we both had a lot of prayers and Office to catch up on. My companion was shocked that I would skip them, and I was infuriated that she'd spend another hour with the light on doing her duty. We were as different as chalk and cheese.

Other than when walking out, two by two was discouraged. No particular friendships allowed. No ears to vent on, no shoulders to cry on, no hearts to share the highs and the lows. I guess silence when walking was to curtail any such activities. There were a few places in the school grounds where a chat could be held beyond prying eyes, but mostly when the need arose they were already occupied.

Two by two was allowed when reciting the rosary. Many a rosary went on for much longer than the ten minutes that it actually took to work one's way around the beads.

Recreation was the time for talking – but with thirty of us around two tables, conversation was very restrained and public. And hands had to be occupied in some form of handiwork, such as mending stockings or making teaching aids.

Two by two extended to having a companion when on study excursions or camps, even if the companion had no knowledge or interest in the subject at hand. I'm not sure how I managed to miss noticing an older novice falling in love with the lecturer on a geography camp that I had to attend with her, but I did.

I passed on the opportunity to visit the great granite outcrops on Eyre Peninsula because it just all seemed too hard in terms of carting someone else up and down their slopes.

However, another roped-in nun and I wandered over every square inch of the Harrison's Creek catchment area on the eastern slopes of the Mount Lofty Ranges when I was studying its geo-morphology for my thesis. By this time we were allowed to go in civvies on such occasions. One evening, a car load of local hoons chased our car for miles, until we thought to drive into someone's home road as if we lived there. I was glad that we were two that time.

When I finally left the convent, I think that the heart of my reason for leaving was about the need to have an intimate relationship with a real person.

Washing Day

Following in every sense of age-old tradition, Monday was washing day in the convent. First-year novices helped the washer-nun do the laundry. Nuns had to wash out their own smalls before consigning them to the machine. How I hated washing out my large white snotty handkerchiefs resulting from my almost constant hay fever. Giant washing machines and driers had to be loaded and unloaded, sheets and things had to be fed through the mangle and received on the other end without getting great tangles around the rollers. Each piece of clothing had a number attached (I think mine was 167) so folding also entailed consigning to numbered piles which were then delivered in big wicker baskets to each nun's room. The baskets were carried by several novices holding one end of a separate basket in each hand, like a camel train.

Coif   *Dimity*

And the starching had to be done. Now, starching was a skill that had to conform to standards of perfection. Coifs and dimities were the objects of this art. Coifs were the collar-like pieces of the habit which were connected to cap-like structures and whose tails were tied under the veil behind the head, while dimities were the smaller pieces of the habit that sat on the forehead pinned to the cap-like structure. These were soaked in starch then smoothed onto huge zinc sheets (rather like giant Rolf Harris wobble boards). It was in the smoothing that the skill lay – every bubble, every crease had to be banished to produce a perfectly flat stiff coif. And dimities needed extra starch so that they didn't collapse on our foreheads in the heat of summer.

As you can imagine, the temptation to starch other things, such as older nuns' bloomers, was overpowering and on at least one occasion we succumbed to it. Large and very flat and very stiff, with not a bubble in them!

The Novices' Picnic

I'm really having trouble remembering the details of this annual trip; however, the broad picture still vividly remains. Once a year, all the novices were taken by bus to the hills property of the well-to-do parents of one of the community sisters, where the owners threw a picnic for us. Two things about it come to mind. Firstly the food, and secondly the boats.

A seemingly never-ending amount of classy picnic food was available, highlighted by an ice cream machine soft-serving an endless supply of the most delicious stuff. We must have gone back to it countless times, for many of us were a pale shade of green and feeling less than well on the way home.

The novice mistress spent the day ensconced inside with the lady of the house and Devonshire tea served on the best china, and perhaps even a port or two, while we (like children) had to remain outside.

A section of the creek had been dammed to form a small lake; rowboats were provided for our use. I don't remember actually falling into the murky water, although the oars certainly did and needed retrieving. By home time, the bottom half of the skirt of my white habit had definitely taken on a grey and grubby hue.

How many chunders do you reckon spewed forth on the way home?

Testing the Boundaries

At university we joined the Catholic student group which met on Thursdays for Mass and discussion. A great forum for debate, argument and apologetics. Thursday was also the special day for the community in the small convent that I lived in when we made an effort to come together from our scattered activities for evening Mass, tea and recreation.

This was the time when theologians were beginning to promote Eucharist as a sign and agent of community over and above the individual value of receiving Christ's body. It was also the time when receiving the Eucharist was allowed only once each day. My dilemma was that I really wanted to express my identity as a member of both the university and religious community by receiving Eucharist at both Masses. So I went to a higher Church authority, the bishop, to ask permission. It wasn't granted, so I went ahead anyway on the authority of my own conscience, and never asked permission for anything again if it wasn't likely to be granted – a practice that I have kept up until this day.

Being part of a group that shared inner thoughts and opinions sometimes called for a one-on-one meeting. The coffee shop at the university was really out of bounds for nuns on several grounds. Firstly, eating or drinking in public wasn't on; and secondly, the vow of poverty ensured that I had no money to even begin to entertain the thought. I tried the mother superior over this one; she understood my missionary zeal and gave me money that I didn't even have to account for.

A Watery End

This is a very short story. The less said of it, the better, really.

As I previously pointed out, some of us were young and immature, still teenagers when we first entered. Sister Stephen and I were on washing up the pots and pans duty one evening while everyone else was at prayers. Somehow we got to chasing each other around the kitchen armed with saucepans of water, only threatening to throw the contents rather than actually doing the deed. We must have been making a bit of a racket, and, unbeknown to us, the novice mistress came to investigate. She was an expert at gliding silently by and coming upon one unawares. She was a bit too quiet on this fateful evening, for when the water was let fly, it was she who copped it.

Hmmm, the less said of it, the better, really!

The Fires of Hell

At one stage, my room was in the north-east corner on the third and top floor of one of the school buildings. Between my room and the bathrooms was one other sister's room. All the other rooms were on the other side of the corridor. On the ground floor right under my window was Siebert Funerals' carpentry shop, where they made the coffins.

In the middle of the night, or perhaps it was the morning for I had studied late into the night, the carpentry shop caught fire, shooting loud explosive sparks and menacing flames high into the air. It was the acrid smell of smoke and piercing crackle of my windowpane that woke me up. Boy, did I panic. I immediately found my glasses and set out at full speed in my nightwear down the corridor and down the stairs. Halfway down the stairs it occurred to me that if I didn't retrieve my just-finished assignment, I would have to do it all over again. So back up the stairs I went and gathered all my study materials, packing them quickly and carefully into my satchel. While I was there I also grabbed my habit and veil so as not to be caught dishabille in the morning. And down the corridor I set out again, wondering why no one else was on the move.

So I retraced my steps again and knocked politely on my neighbour's door. She was out of bed by this stage, so together we woke the other twenty sisters who also slept on the third floor. They had heard nothing, being that much further removed from the action than we were. And then there was a stampede down the stairs.

By now the wail of sirens could be heard getting closer. Hosing water caused mountains of steam as if from volcanic hot springs. It was all over quite quickly, really, with no damage to the school building except a few broken windows and singed windowpanes. But the carpentry shop had been reduced to a pile of smouldering timbers dumped between four bare walls.

The smell of smoke hung around for days. Every time I woke on the following nights, I could smell it. And if my eye caught the weather beacon on top of the *Advertiser* building red-flashing for a storm, I was halfway down the stairs again as quick as a flash imagining the worst. I was sure we were given a minuscule forewarning of what hell might entail and hoped that it wasn't indicative for the dead people for whom the coffins were made.

Creative Endeavours

Everybody got to be creative in quite amazing ways in the convent. Making teaching aids was a popular pastime for teachers at recreation. During our afternoon and evening recreation periods we couldn't just sit and yack (beware of gossiping!). The maxim 'The devil makes work for idle hands' was strongly instilled, so darning our thick black stockings was a fairly constant activity.

The vow of poverty precluded us from having money, full stop, let alone buying gifts for anyone. It was a constant challenge to make or find something for the other twenty-nine novices on their feast days. Those who celebrated in the rose-blooming season were certain to receive enough single pilfered roses to make whole bouquets. Those who could draw and paint and those who could write poetry were certainly well endowed for gift-giving.

This poem I gave to a sister named for St Joseph.

On the feast of St Joseph

> One had pitched his tent within
> before the spring had come.
> And he was filled with confusion.
> Fear not
> it is the anointed one.

Finding presents for family at Christmas and birthdays also stretched the imagination. In days long before patchwork became a popular art form, we undertook our own forms of sewing with small scraps of material, creating quite beautiful but useless things. One year I made my mother a book with great images and quotations to try and explain the vows I had taken. The painting from the cover is reproduced on the front of this book – it features the table of the altar, the chi-rho (PX) and the fish and candle signs for Christ, and the arches of the convent cloisters.

Christmas

In one of my novitiate years I got very creative for Christmas. I made a 'stained glass' nativity scene out of cellophane paper pasted behind cardboard that was painted black with the various shapes cut out. It was quite large, probably about a metre and a half by a metre, and I stuck it on the west-facing refectory window where the setting sun turned it into an ever-changing thing of beauty. It took a long time to scrounge enough bits of cellophane and to experiment with combining different coloured pieces to obtain the perfect hue for each 'glass' section. I kept it hidden in my room during its creation. My room was very messy for a couple of months so I had to be careful not to open the door too wide on the way in and out lest I was sprung.

That same Christmas, I collected bits and pieces for what I called my sixty-four-sided square. This nomenclature referred to the box in which I collected the materials for a bonbon for each of the sixty-four sisters in the house at the time. Sixty-four bonbons called for sixty-four toilet roll innards and a couple of hundred articles to go inside. The paper hats and jokes were easy enough to make but very small knick-knacks were harder to come by legitimately. Lollies, beautiful little shells, cedar rose seed pods, holy cards, small soaps, smooth and varnished beach pebbles…

The long holidays

Uni holidays were long, at least three months. The question of what were the uni student nuns going to do in this time came up every year. One year we were put to work in the school library to help classify all the books with a Dewey number. At the end of the year that my uni companion and I had studied geology, we were given the task of identifying all the unclassified bits and pieces in the school science laboratory geology collection, and to build the collection with multiple copies of each rock. This entailed poring over rocks with penknives to test hardness and magnifying glasses to inspect minute specks, and consulting reference books to augment our knowledge. It also entailed fieldwork, a legitimate way of escaping the conventual confines. So we traipsed over the countryside in our habits, armed with geology picks, and came home with boxes of rocks. Marble was quite easy to come by – a few small stones every time we passed a cemetery soon provided enough samples for our purpose. We also had to call in professional help for what we couldn't manage with our new knowledge.

During another long break, I studied musical theory with the help of one of the older nun musical teachers, and decided to sit the exam for fourth grade. I remember learning the meaning of musical terms while walking down to Bonython Hall for the exam. I did recall enough of them to pass. I always was a last-minute person. Out of this endeavour came one memorable song, 'Song of Isaias', which was widely sung throughout Adelaide in the years after I left the convent and was recorded by Sister Janet Mead of the 'Our Father' fame.

In the Wind

The order I belonged to had houses all over the countryside, including several in the south-east of the state. We city sisters had very few opportunities to meet and to get to know our country sisters. Personally I lamented this state of affairs, and set about getting support to produce a newsletter cum magazine that I hoped might bridge the gap a little. It contained all sorts of things from a personality corner wherein individual sisters shared something of their lives, to theological discussions in the wake of Vatican II, and even to recipes tried and true. I called it *In the Wind*, and the wind blew for many years after I left.

Erindale Easter

In my last year, I lived in a large old house that was the convent at Erindale. We still went into the mother house for the official ceremonies of the Easter liturgy, but for the other celebrations we did our own thing. I had volunteered to lead the Stations of the Cross at Erindale on Good Friday morning. Not, as was the custom, in the chapel, for our chapel was the tiny front room where walking the Way of the Cross consisted of about two steps between each station, but outside in the large and sprawling grounds of the Erindale property. We gathered near some part of the landscape that was evocative for each station (like the huge oak tree, a spiky peace rose, the dry creek, the pillared side entrance) and listened to poignant and popular music, reflections and poetry that picked up the mood of the various stations. Simon and Garfunkel, Peter, Paul and Mary, and Bob Dylan were 'in' at the time. Some of the nuns were moved to tears.

Ah yes, and dancing under the full moon on the crisp clear autumn night after coming home from the Easter Saturday Vigil celebrations will never be forgotten. Even the most staid of sisters joined in. Great Silence came late that night!

Vatican II

Even before I entered the convent, the initial sessions of the Second Vatican Council had been held in Rome. The fourth and last session was held at the end of 1965. Pope John XXIII had called the council together in order to modernise the Church and open a dialogue with other religions. He spoke of 'opening the windows' to allow the winds of change that were blowing throughout the world to renew the Church from the inside out. However, it was only slowly that new theological perspectives seeped through to Catholics all over the world.

Some of the Documents of Vatican II were read to us at meal times (far less gory than the Martyrology). But it was difficult to concentrate on such weighty matters while eating our meal.

The *Constitution on the Sacred Liturgy* was issued at the end of 1963. The first set of instructions on its implementation came out about a year later. And so gradually the priest began to face the people and English replaced Latin as the language of the Mass. Later still, modern music began to be composed and sung (including my 'Song of Isaias'). All to ensure that the faithful participated more fully in the liturgy.

Best of all, the rites of Easter were revised, and we no longer had to sing all the Latin Gregorian chant that we spent hours practising as novices. And we did the ceremonies so well that Easter was all that it could be – a real resurrection. I remember being deeply disappointed at my first Easter outside the convent.

While the *Decree on the Up-to-date Renewal of Religious Life* was issued late in 1965, the more detailed *Instruction on the Renewal of Religious Life* didn't emerge until 1969. Even then, the details of changes in day-to-day life were not spelt out in these documents, but left for each order

55

to nut out the practical meanings for themselves. And these processes all took several years.

Some small changes in religious life had begun to appear in my later years there.

Certainly our dress code changed. Habits and veils were shortened and made of lighter material. You could even see our legs and hair! Civvies could be worn on appropriate occasions: I remember wearing a blouse and skirt while clambering all over the landscape at Harrison's Creek doing fieldwork for my thesis, but I'm not sure where they came from. I certainly had no civvies hanging in my wardrobe at any time.

Closer relations with our families were encouraged. Instead of family members visiting us once a month on a Sunday afternoon, we could go home for special occasions, including Christmas tea.

I think we might have been allowed to walk out by ourselves. How else could I have gotten away with missing Benediction and confession every Friday afternoon for a couple of years? Certainly my student companion sister would not have been accessory to the fact. I just simply couldn't see the point of Benediction, or of such frequent confession when we weren't living a life of crime.

One of the major results of imbibing the new-found freedoms of Vatican II was that a whole lot of sisters left convents – I was one of the first of this exodus in our order.

Dying Embers

During my sixth year in the convent and my third year as a professed community sister, I was doing Honours at the university and living in one of the smaller convents rather than the large mother house where the five previous years had been lived out. This was a good year. I no longer had to live in my student companion's pocket; she had completed her degree and was teaching somewhere far away.

The house was a two-storey one, set in large and rambling grounds, far more conducive to meditation on the few occasions I managed to stay awake. The sitting room had a real live fireplace fed in the winter from the never-ending woodpile out the back.

Much soul-sharing, philosophising and solving of the world's problems went on while waiting for the fire to die at night and poking the dying embers through the grate. Mind you, by reclaiming the fire just one more time with an extra log, this process could be quite an extended one. And Great Silence didn't seem to be such an issue by then.

Life was different at this house. With only half a dozen of us, a much more normal regime could flourish, at least in terms of housekeeping and relationships, even if not in the area of the daily timetable.

Aggiornamento following Vatican II had already begun to pervade the practice of religious life. One of the new and hopefully life-giving aspects was a consciousness of the value of not only life and prayer in common but also of sharing and articulating together the faith dimensions underpinning our life. Previously life was lived because it had always been done that way (probably for at least a thousand years for nuns in general, and certainly for nearly a couple of hundred years since the foundation of our order). Thank goodness that view of life was dying.

You have no doubt picked up by now that all along I had a healthy disrespect for rules and codes of behaviour that held little meaning for me.

But when it came to sharing faith I discovered that everyone else's life was based on a loving and intimate relationship with God, and articulated in such a way that I was not able to discern the presence of this vital ingredient in my own experience. I wrestled with this absence, envied it in others, longed that it would be likewise for me, sought ways to bring it into my life, but was seemingly unable not only to acquire it by any means but also to articulate coherently all of this turmoil.

They got the message about the turmoil but were unable to understand it or accept it. Pithy little sayings like 'Let go and let God', 'Restless are our hearts until…' began to be bandied about and poem pictures called Footsteps began to be an oft-repeated gift for even the slightest excuse for an occasion. These were about as helpful as the current saying 'Been there, done that' trotted out by people whose children were one stage ahead of mine at any given time. Certainly a wipe-off.

The dying embers remind me dramatically of the night when I was just a new community sister, having recently sloughed the chrysalis of the novitiate, and was given the charge of sitting through the night with one of the older sisters who was dying. She was spluttering for breath, and heaving her whole frame in the effort to draw in sufficient air to prevent a total shutdown of her respiratory system. It was frightening at the time. My first close encounter with death. I rosaried for her frantically. 'Holy Mary, pray for her now, at this hour of her death.' She didn't seem to be listening, neither Holy Mary nor Sister Rose. Eventually in the dead of the night, when I could no longer envisage how I might handle the worsening situation or if she actually did the dying deed, I woke others up to join me.

Weeks later, I wrote a long poem on the whole episode, but being new to the craft and considering what I had written was sloppy and sentimental, most of it got ditched. A few lines remain.

Lines from Opus 2

The night was heavy.
Her candle, her Light, flickered.
Ghostly shadows danced on the wall.
Her flesh was cold
cold
cold as a tombstone.
...
Again silence
the gentle flow of life forced through a tube...
...
And I thought of life and remembered death
for what is life but a prologue to death
and what is death but a beginning of life.
I am the resurrection and the life
they who believe in me though they are dead
will live on. (October 1966)

By the way, Sister Rose calmed down at dawn, had a peaceful and alert morning, and slipped away quietly in the early afternoon while I was sleeping it off.

This wasn't the first time since that fateful morning when I entered that I considered the possibility of leaving religious life. Fairly regularly, the futility of ever learning humility and obedience had propelled me into such thoughts.

In my imagination I had once or twice stood back from the life I was living and viewed it from the outside, coming to the conclusion that no sane person would willingly choose such a life. 'The Madman' poem was written while staying at the Goodwood Orphanage at a time when all its children were away on holidays – a large hollow empty echo-resounding shell with a pigeon problem visible in the ever-present droppings that speckled three storeys of balconies and windowsills.

Song of a Madman

I live in thair
all dai long
an doan go oud at nite
an I gedup erly
to say me prairs
an the pijins
cum home at nite
to roost
an in the morning
they coo at me
Coo-oo, coo-oo (May 1967)

Get behind me, Satan! Such thoughts are but pride. Humility must be victorious. I never really got to checking out the novice mistress's and later the mother superior's reaction to a request from me to leave. In some ways I didn't fit the pattern of those who'd left before me – mostly people who didn't seem to cope with a community way of living or were obsessive about the rules. Ultimately I was in the vanguard of the great exodus that happened in the wake of Vatican II. The freedom to choose. It gave those who stayed the freedom to choose the life rather than to be bound by it.

When I finally convinced the powers-that-be that outside was more appropriate for me, I was counselled to stay the three months remaining of my period of vows – how much easier it would be than going through the process of applying to Rome for a dispensation, and it would probably take that long anyway. I acquiesced, for important exams were coming up and a thesis had to be completed.

But a geography camp with fellow university students really emphasised the impossibility of the lie of living in it but not of it, and so I left promising to continue to live out the vows in the wide world until their due date expired. Not really a very difficult task – I wasn't about to jump into some fellow's bed that soon.

Some ten to fifteen years later, during an extended period of 'conversion', the realisation dawned that what I thought I didn't have and could never have in the faith realm was in fact not only possible for me, but growing before my eyes, and I was revelling in it. With it came anger that no one had bothered to empower me into such a relationship at the time of leaving. Accompanying resentment was fanned in those new embers too, and for a short time I wanted to prove that I could have made it, by having another go. However, by then firmly entrenched in family life, that was not an option at all and gradually that fire too died down. And was replaced by a new valuing of the lay Christian life as more than a second-class option.

On the playground at Goodwood. Note the sleeves tucked in at the apron's waistline.

The Question of Why (Again)

Many factors were probably influential in my decision to leave the convent. You will have noticed that I had certain difficulties in keeping the rules all along, but these in themselves were not the reason I left. And while on many occasions from the very beginning I was tempted to leave, I had been too scared of the novice mistress to put my case to her. Most of those who left the novitiate before me were either social misfits or they had very strange attitudes to the rules, like one for whom we made a 'bligger tree' because she would continually inquire as to whether what she was required to do was obligatory or not.

Certainly I wasn't asked to leave at any stage. Quite the contrary. When the time came, I had great difficulty in convincing the superiors that I ought to leave. I had proven to be a halfway decent teacher, got on with most of the other sisters and contributed significantly and creatively to community life.

I found it quite difficult to articulate that I wanted to leave in order to pursue a relationship with some special person that was more real than my relationship with God. I was sent from pillar to post to explain yet again why I wanted to go, even to a local pastorally minded priest who tried very hard to convince me to stay. None of these people made any effort to help me to change or improve my relationship with God to make it a more life-giving one, and in the end they reluctantly let me go.

And as a postscript, just in case you were thinking it to be so, this decision had nothing at all to do with sex!

And so, one day, very early in the morning, my parents picked me up and, like all those before me, I went without saying goodbye. The only sister who knew I was leaving was the one who made me a blouse and a skirt, my one outfit of clothing to wear on the outside.

Postscript

On looking back at the whole convent experience, I would have to say that, except for my failures in the spiritual realm, it was 'all good', as my children would quip.

I really appreciated and contributed to community life. I recognised within myself and cultivated a creativity of many dimensions. I discovered a modicum of self-confidence which soon evaporated in the unknown of the outside world. I came to a whole new understanding of Church and its role in our lives and in the modern world, and I gained a new appreciation for good liturgy. I made some lasting friends and, in the more practical realm, I learnt to drive and gained a university degree.

In short, I graduated from being a gawky country bumpkin of a girl to becoming a young woman with developing maturity, like a soft red wine or a smooth Camembert. Yes, it was good.

Post Postscript

Convent life today, of course, is nothing like it was in my time. Nuns – no, religious sisters – live normal lives nowadays.

CPSIA information can be obtained
at www.ICGtesting.com
Printed in the USA
BVHW01s0613160218
508105BV00001B/116/P